The Gospel

AND

The Sword

For information contact:
info@uptownmediaventures.com

Book and Cover design by Tim White Publishing

ISBN: 978-1-68121-112-1

10 9 8 7 6 5 4 3 2 1

Table of Contents

Introduction   5

The Eviction   9

Morals   19

No Peace   27

Two-Edged Sword   35

Come Out Wherever You Are   45

The Gospel   49

Radical Relationship   55

The War is On!   59

The Whole Armor of God   65

Trouble in the Valley   81

Conclusion   85

About the Author   87

Introduction

As believers in the body of Christ we are instructed to put on the whole armor of God, as if we have been drafted and recruited for military service. We are additionally told that our battle is not one of flesh and blood, although the enemy uses flesh and blood individuals, to get his agenda across.

We are at war, it is spiritual warfare, and what's at stake is man's very soul.

We will in part look at Paul's letter to the Ephesian church as he wanted them to be aware that they would not be wrestling (battling, warring, and fighting) against flesh and blood powers.

Consider this; all aggression begins with thoughts that lead to intent and ultimately physical confrontation and altercations.

If only all these battles could remain spiritual, there would be no loss of human lives, sadly that would not be the case.

If only we could get people to just feel better about themselves, or about the world around them there would be no wars, no fighting or death. Man is competitive and enjoys seeing the results of his work, and to know what he has done has had an effect on those he wants to rule and have dominion over.

Maybe if we could convince people they are not bad, rebellious or evil they might possibly turn over a new leaf and become better and more productive citizens on this planet we call earth. If we can just make them feel good they will only want to do good as well.

Maybe the gospel is too harsh, and some people don't need to hear all that fire and brimstone and talk of Hell. God is the God of love and he does not want us to spend our time talking about people going to a place of torment and eternal pain, but, hell as just as real as Heaven.

This is the dawn of a new generation we are being told, a more enlightened age when we should all just try to get alone. We no longer view things as sinful or even call sin what it is, sin.

Things are just an inconvenience, a small misunderstanding or a difference of personal views. There are two radically different views as it pertains to peace, the external and the internal. We will show how these oppose one another. We seek both, but often end up with neither.

Sin suggests that we are less than perfect, that we have the nature as well as the potential to do evil things. You can find the use of the word evil, but not sin.

There is talk of prayer but never to whom because we don't want to offend, or exclude anyone's religious practice including Satan. The world is turning more towards secular humanism and that we are all the same.

Although the gospel is good news, it is also a divider, it's a sword for battle, and once it is strapped on you need to make ready. If you are not sure of its use this book might help. It's time to stop giving out a candy coated gospel that's sweet and tickles the ears of the listeners, sure it makes for great swelling congregations, but it does not mean heaven bound, it's emotionally satisfying, but not spiritually fulfilling.

It's time to stop only feeling good and start doing good as well. We will delve into and explore what Jesus meant when he said, **think not that I am come to send peace on earth, not peace, but a sword.**

A sword was not a symbol of peace but of conquering. There are variations on swords; they come in different sizes as well as shapes, often to fit the owner's specific taste. The sword is found in most cultures dating back thousands of years, and called by many names.

Swords served a dual purpose, they were used for self-defense and for the defense of another, but make no mistake about it, swords were created to inflict harm or death to the one it is used on. Swords (and daggers) were the guns of ancient times, the sword made killing very personal since it was done at close range.

Many soldiers in the military in the past had certain equipment as part of their uniforms, and we will talk more about a few types of them later in this book.

A soldier's uniform was not complete if he did not have a sword, a dagger, and the pilum (or spear), as their main weapons. There is another weapon that is not often seen or spoken of as well. It was that nails were driven into the sole of sandals (called Caliga), to help improve grip, but they were also used to inflict additional harm on their fallen enemy. Some of these items we will examine closer in this writing of the Gospel and the sword.

The Eviction

The first mention of sword is found in the book of Genesis. It comes at the point of man's sin and he is no longer allowed to be in the Garden of Eden. The Lord drove them out of the garden and placed Cherubim's (one order of angels, we will speak more of them later), and a flaming sword that turned in every direction blocking the tree of Life (Genesis.3: 24).

A sword denotes power of life and death, protection and judgment as well; we will be talking more about this throughout the course of the book.

Why was it that Adam (and Eve), was served an eviction notice from God, and driven from the only home they had known? All he had done was eat of the fruit that was given to him by his wife. As with anything in life there are rules or guidelines that should be followed. God being the owner and Creator, gave Adam **only one commandment** (rule, guideline) to obey (follow); let's call it Adams lease agreement.

Adam was instructed by the Lord God that he could freely eat of every tree in the garden, all but one, the tree of the knowledge of good and evil, warning him also that the day he would do so he would surely die (Genesis.2: 17).

God allowed Adam to live in the most beautiful home on earth created by the Lord God for his creation, Adam even had exclusive access to the penthouse (Heaven), where he saw angels coming and going all the time, even having Christ himself as a visitor to the garden to walk and talk to him.

One would ask, what else could he have possibly needed, Adam not only could see Heaven, but experience it as well, from his home in the garden. He had the life that many are seeking today, the experience of a lifetime. What would make a man give up such a place as this, what would motivate such an action?

I know we have been very critical of Adam, many of us would never do what he did, at least so we say. How could the man who had everything give it all up? If that were me some dare to say, they would never do what Adam did.

Let's understand something here; Adam did not have the nature of sin, but a nature to sin. Let me explain what I mean by this. Adam was not the offspring of anyone before him, he did not have parents who were sinners, Adam's parent was the Lord God, Adam was not born at all, but created by the hand of God, and Adam was not born with a sin nature as you and I were, this however, did not mean he could not sin, if he chose to do so, (*and would*). In other words, **Adam could sin if he chose to, not because he had to**. In the book of Romans, we learn, all have sinned and come short of the glory (holiness) of God (Romans.3: 23).

David said, behold I was shapen in iniquity, and in sin did my mother conceive me (Psalms.51: 5).

Was Adam's immorality Eve's fault, was the woman the reason for all mankind's ills? Was she the cause of their eviction from Eden? When man was placed in the Garden of Eden the Lord God only gave one commandment (rule), a simple instruction to abide by and easy to do, don't eat of the tree of good and evil.

There is something about being told not to do something that somehow challenges us to see what would happen if we did it. Some have called it curiosity, a need to know, a strong desire to see what would transpire.

People do not honestly weigh the consequences of their curiosity; "it can't be that bad" is what often motivates the individual.

We have mentioned the word sin a number of times. Maybe we should define what sin is before we continue. I will keep this simple, **Adams sin, WAS DISOBEDIENCE**, it was the rejection of a specific teaching from God.

In the book of Romans, we find these words, for as by one man's (Adam's) disobedience many were made sinners, so by the obedience of one (Christ) shall many be made righteous (Romans.5: 19).

Those without Christ are also called the children of disobedience (Ephesians. 2: 2; 5: 8).

A perfect home is about to be changed forever by what seemed like a harmless act by Adam. The home he once knew would soon be shut off to him, and would be seen ever more at a distance, and would quickly be gone from his physical eyesight. This eviction from Eden would have consequences that Adam and Eve could never have imagined.

Adam's sin was a willing sin. Hebrews.10: 26 says, *if we sin willingly after we have received the knowledge (teaching) of the truth, there remains no more sacrifice for sin.*

In other words, God is not going to keep sending His Son to die again and again for our sins. From the cross of Calvary, we hear the words of our Lord when he declared right before dying, "it is finished", (John.19: 30). This cry lets us know that the final offering was now accepted by God, none will follow. God gave Christ to the world, his only begotten Son.

What did it mean to be excommunicated from Eden, what would happen to Adam and his wife, maybe there was a chance they could convince God to give them another chance, it was just a simple misunderstanding?

Man's innocence was now gone, it was lost to sin, Adam violated the simple command to obey, opening the door to his own destruction, disobedience is also the rejection of Love, the childlike obedience and innocence has now given way to disobedience, and selfishness, and these are things that cannot remain in the presence, or house of God which was Eden at that time.

Lucifer's sin of wanting to be like God, was what caused him to be cast (evicted) from Heaven (Isaiah.14: 12-14), and now in the Garden of Eden by his prompting, the serpent challenged man to doubt and question Gods word, and authority. (Bear in mind that Satan did not make either Eve or Adam sin, he only tempted them to do so, the act of sin was by their own choice).

This eviction from the Garden was not random, it did not just happen, it was a process, and certain things had to take place first. There were things that led up to it.

If someone signs a lease they have to agree to terms and conditions in that lease, or it can be considered violated, its terms become null, and if it's broken by one or another of the parties involved, it's considered void.

First, Eve had a conversation with someone who suggested that she had been lied to, that God was hiding or keeping them from knowing certain things, and that if she ate of the tree she could become like God.

Satan will use one of three methods to get his point across to us, and all of them can lead to sin.

In the book of I John we find these words, *love not the world neither the things that are of the world, if any man loves the world the love of the Father is not in him, for all that is in the world, the lust of the flesh, and the lust of the eyes, and the pride of life, is not of the Father, but is of the world, and the world passeth away and the lust thereof, but he that doeth the will of God abideth for ever* (I John.2: 15-17).

Eve was caught up with what the Lord God told them not to do, forgetting about all He gave them to enjoy, and could do. It always seems that the one thing we are told we can't have, or should not bother, almost becomes our single focus to obtain.

The eviction process had begun with the mind of Eve. In Genesis 3: 6 we find all three aspects of sin we spoke of, go in effect with Eve. The **lust of the**

flesh, the **lust of the eyes,** and the **pride of life**. Her choice was as simple as, obey or disobey.

I Timothy 2:14 says the woman was deceived, she was misled and seduced by the doctrine of the serpent, Eve's emotions played her, but Adam was not deceived, and because of his willingness to disobey, the Lord God had to serve them an eviction notice. Let's be mindful that the man is the head of the woman (I Corinthians.11: 3).

Disobedience has to be disciplined, but being a loving Father, The Lord allowed them to have their say as to what happened.

The Lord gave them their day in his court to plead their case. Would they be honest and tell the truth?

Eve blamed the serpent, Adam took his complaint all the way to the top, and Adam blamed God, saying the woman whom he gave to be with him basically tricked him (Genesis.3: 12). Instead of owning up to what was done everyone passed the proverbial buck.

Adam's name was on the lease not only for the Garden of Eden but for the whole world, he had been given the rule (Dominion) over every living creature that the Lord God had created (Genesis.1: 28).

Adam's position was that of being just a little lower than angels since God created the angels before man, according to Psalms.8: 1-9. Bear in mind that this does not mean angels are better than man; they are different from man, in what the Lord had created them to do. That's for another book it would take more time than we have here to speak on it.

Adam disobeyed God, and for that, he would no longer be allowed to remain in the Garden of paradise. Man's relationship had changed; the death (spiritually), the Lord had spoken of had now taken place, and the physical death would follow. We must understand a little more about the death as it was spoken of here. Death is in three parts.

The first death they experienced, was a spiritual death; it comes from separation from God. Adam's sin caused them to hide from the Lord (Genesis.3: 8-10). Sin will make God a stranger to us, and distant. Sin causes people to move further and further away from God, even to the place of seeing God as nonexistent to them.

Adam had lost his lease, the deed, and partnership, and would have to depart from the Garden; Adam had in effect given the world's lease to Satan, who with great pride, received it gladly.

Satan wanted what man had, and did what he had to do **to get it freely from Adam.**

Corruption could not be allowed to remain in the Garden no more than it was allowed to remain in Heaven. Adam and Eve had to leave the Garden of delight, the paradise the Lord God had prepared for them, but God loved them and also gave them hope and a promise, just as today he told us he would not leave us comfortless and would send the Holy Spirit of promise on the day of Pentecost (John.14: 15-26; Acts.2: 1-4; Ephesians.1: 1-13).

Adam was reassured by the Lord that things would work out okay in spite of what happened, **Satan had the deed to the earth by forfeiture**, it legally belonged to Satan, but the Lord already had a plan to get it back, to redeem it. The first words of prophecy are spoken to Adam and Eve in Genesis 3: 15 letting them know what future event would take place to bring about the cure for what had taken place in the Garden.

Now, let's continue to examine the matter of death. Nothing had died before, so, it was not something that was familiar to Adam when the Lord God spoke it to him.

A transformation was already taking place inside them, they knew things were different the moment they sinned, it was the very reason they hid themselves.

Death takes place on three levels. The first **1)** death is spiritual as we have seen, it is the running and hiding one's self from the judgment that is known or understood to follow, and it's a conscious awareness.

The direct fellowship they had with God was severed being blocked by sin, and access to Heaven changed. **2)** the second aspect of death, it is physical, sin has shortened our days on earth, Adam was 930 years old when he died (Genesis.5: 5), Noah was 950 when he died (Genesis.9: 29), Abraham was 175 years old when he died (Genesis.25: 7), Moses was 120 years old at his death (Deuteronomy.34: 7), today its big news if someone lives to be over 100 years old, sin has shortened our days.

Our lives are as a vapor that one moment you see it and the next it's gone (James.4: 14), and **3)** third, the last aspect of death is the eternal death the time when body and soul is destroyed in the lake of fire, for those without Christ.

Adam and Eve were put out of the Garden but was always in God's sight. The battle had begun for the soul of man since Satan was given the lease to the earth by Adam.

Adam's rebellion put God's plan of redemption into full force, and we now have a battle of Good and Evil that is waged for man's soul. It's time to get equipped for the war that is upon us, by putting on the whole armor provided by God.

Morals

In spite of what we would like to believe, the word of God was not written to make friends, it was not given to make us comfortable and it is not spoken that people would think they are okay. God gave his word that it would let us know, that we are sick creatures in need of a physician, and that we are like lost sheep needing a shepherd.

Man (including woman) is a wicked person with a tendency to do evil but capable of doing good things. Headlines greet us almost daily bearing this out, how family after family is being torn apart because of some evil deed done. Some horrendous act of violence, rape, murder, drugs and suicide. All on the increase, with seemingly nothing that is done or seems to work to control it.

Millions of dollars are being paid to study the cause of such incidences and their contributing factors. When there is no order chaos ensues. Is this an environmental issue, could it be some experience of trauma that possibly brought about these actions?

Man's actions are determined by his conscience, his choice, and his willingness to choose evil over good morals. Let's again refer back to ORIGINAL MAN (Adam).

Adam was created innocent, just like a baby, and as intelligent as he was, he was still only a child. I know that's a hard pill to swallow, given Adam had the knowledge to name all the animals, and was given dominion over them, that does not seem like the authority anyone would give a child.

There was nothing wild, nothing harmful, all creation was docile, there was no fear of creatures and there was no death to concern them with, it was like putting a child in his playpen today. All creatures were vegetarian until after the flood (Genesis.1: 29; 9: 1-4).

Bear in mind that Man is a conscience (thinking), creature. The Lord God equipped man to be able to reason, it's why He said, let us make man in our image after our likeness (Genesis.1: 26).

This does not mean Adam looked like God, but that he had the capacity to reason, to think, and choose like his creator. Note: God did not create man to be like a robot without a mind, a will, and emotion. Or to blindly follow and obey him, to do so would not demonstrate love.

God seeks man's love on a voluntary basis; we love him because he first loved us (I John.4: 19). Love is not true love if it's forced. True love is not fearful. Perfect (mature, spiritual) love, cast out fear (I John.4: 18).

The word of God is filled with practical applications that can be implemented by anyone who has the surrendered will, and mind to do so.

When Adam sinned, he was not given a book to sit down and read, or an instruction manual to memorize. His innocence was gone, and **Adam would now have to be guided by moral standards**, this would become increasingly more difficult in time, because his relationship with God had changed. Sin, (rebellion) now blocks but does not stop his efforts. Adam was instructed what he and his offspring had to do to please God, now that he had become a sinner.

Something had to die to cover man's sin, and this would continue to be so until the Lord Jesus Christ would come and die for man's sin, God's ultimate offering.

The Lord God set the standard for acceptance. God would accept an offering presented to him by their hands, and this would be their way of showing the Lord reverence.

What we have learned here is, that there was no bible as their guide, God's word was placed in their hearts by faith, and their obedience would be seen by their actions.

Everything they did, they would have to do as an act of faith, *without faith the scriptures tell us, it is impossible to please him* (Hebrews.11: 6).

Shortly we will see what is meant by evil communications corrupts good manners (I Corinthians.15: 33) as was the case with Cain.

Morals are subconscious laws or rules that govern the conscious actions based on the respect for others.

Later we find this added to the Law, as given by the Lord to Moses (the Law had three parts, **1**) the MORAL, **2**) the CIVIL and **3**) the CEREMONIAL laws, some 613 laws in all.

Loving God is more than just doing what you are told. The first test of moral obedience came as the brothers Cain and Abel presented their offering to the Lord.

Morals mean nothing if there's no respect for others, who they are, or for what they have.

Morals can be seen as values, or worth. When someone is said to have no morals, it suggests they don't care, they have no respect for anything, or anyone.

Part of Adams duty was to instill moral values in his children. To teach them what the Lord expected from them in life, and when it was time for them to present their sin offering to him, how it should be done.

Does the teaching of godly principles mean it will be met with success, not at all, not all the time and not with everyone?

Adam's two sons became old enough to present their on offerings before the Lord, and when the time came, they did so. But things did not go quite as expected.

The Lord accepted Abel's offering and rejected his brothers, Cain's offering.

Cain was a tiller of the land and Abel raised a flock. Was there something special about Abel's offering that the Lord accepted his above his brother? Some have said that God accepted Abel's offering because it was a blood offering, whereas Cain brought the fruit of the land.

The Lord was not looking at the offering, but rather at the heart of the one making the offer, **it wasn't about what they brought but rather what they thought.**

Scripture shows us that offerings could be made to the Lord from crops (Leviticus.2:1-16 ;), as well as blood offerings (Leviticus.4: 13-17).

The Lord accepted Abel's offering simply because his heart was sincere and he gave it out of love, he was willingly obedient to the Lord, and how do we know this to be true? Look closely at the conversation the Lord had with Cain, and it sheds some light on what happened inside Cain's head morally.

Cain's offering was given out of duty; he gave it because he had to, not because he wanted to. Obedience is a willing desire.

Cain's morals were compromised by his own conscience, he was being faced with a moral dilemma, a mental crisis, his own unwillingness to do what was required of him, and so, what does he do?

The word of God tells us that instead of doing what was required of him, Cain does the unthinkable, and murders his brother (Genesis.4: 8).

Why would he do such a thing, his brother had done nothing to him to provoke him to such an action? Cain was emotionally led, and he was influenced by Satan.

Cain was very angry with God, but since he could not see God, he did the next best (worst) thing, he kills his own brother who God showed favor by accepting his offering.

Being morally led, one would have to as we said earlier, have respect for others. The first murder takes place because of a poor attitude, pride and envy.

Pride goes before destruction and a haughty spirit before the fall (Proverbs.16: 18).

Did Cain know that murder was wrong? Most certainly, not only did he kill his brother, but it appears that he planned it; the evil had taken root in Cain's heart, and had now brought forth fruit.

In the book of I John.3: 12 we learn that Cain was of the evil one (Satan), and that he murdered his brother because his works (deeds, thoughts) were evil.

There was neither remorse nor repentance for what Cain had done, when asked by God where his brother was, he dared to question Almighty God, AM I MY BROTHERS KEEPER (Genesis.4: 9), today it might be said, "I don't keep up with him" or "how should I know", or even "you're God and you mean you don't know?".

Cain's only concern when the Lord revealed to him that he knew what was done to his brother was, what people would do to him if they found out what he had done.

Being moral does not make anyone righteous, but it does put them in a better position to become so.

Being moralistic does not grant anyone access to heaven, Cain's conscience was seared (branded) with a hot iron like Paul told Timothy those who would not accept Christ would be, and even giving heed (listening) to seducing spirits and doctrines (teachings) of devils (I Timothy.4: 1-2).

Today we can find people who don't know Christ, they operate on the moral principles and values of life. Moral people respect life (for the most part), and the laws that govern the land. They respect locks on doors, and the property of others, by not stealing or taking what does not belong to them.

Do we need the bible to be moral people? Not at all, morals are built into each of us, they are strengthened or weakened by those we trust and believe in, physically and spiritually. But understand this also, **the bottom line is choice**, good or evil. Adam had to choose, Eve had to choose, Cain had to choose, and even Lucifer had to choose which direction he would take.

Morals help direct the conscious by our choosing for ourselves if we will do good, or if we will do evil, but it will be our actions that proves our hearts.

No Peace

Peace I leave you, my peace I give unto you, not as the world giveth, give I unto you, let not your heart be troubled neither let it be afraid (John.14: 27).

What a remarkable statement made by Christ. He is facing death in only a few hours and he talks about peace. In fact, this is the first mention of peace recorded in John's gospel, first of only five.

These words were spoken in the upper room as Jesus was preparing for the last supper he would have with his disciples on earth before his death.

As Jesus was facing, and preparing for the cross, he wanted to assure and reassure his disciples of some of the things to come, some things they would all have to likewise face. What they would have to face would require an internal spiritual peace, to get through.

There would be situational hardships to come for each of them, their faith would be tried, and their humanity would be put on full display for the world to see.

Jesus spoke of his relationship with his Father (John.14: 19-25), He and the Father were one in their purpose and mission.

Jesus reminds the disciples just as the Father was with him, he would also be with the disciples as well. In fact, the Father, the Son, and the Comforter (the Holy Spirit), would become a threefold cord that could not be broken in the disciples lives (compare Ecclesiastes.4: 12).

Christ reminded them of the promise of the comforter he would send to them (John.14: 16, 26), and that the comforter would be the one who would continue to teach them once Jesus goes back to the Father.

The Holy Spirit would bring all things to memory that JESUS SAID to them.

Jesus' words were spoken to comfort the disciples, but these words also came as a warning, the peace Jesus was referring to should not be compared to the peace that the world speaks of.

Zophar, a man who thought to reprimand Job on God's behalf, believed Job's condition was brought on by sin, (*too often there are people who think they are speaking on God's behalf, when they should not be speaking at all*). Job lets Zophar know that he should not be so quick to speak, but to hold his peace (Job.13: 13), in other words shut up.

This was not the peace Jesus was referring to, although Jesus does let the disciples know, that the time would come that believers should hold their peace, and it would be given to them what to say by the Holy Spirit when it was time (Matthew.10: 19-22).

Holding one's peace simply means, to remain silent. Jesus did this as he stood before the high priest (Mark.14: 58-61).

There is also what was known as a peace offering (Leviticus.3: 1-17; 7: 12-17).

It served several purposes; it was for thanksgiving, deliverance, answer to prayer, healing, and even for something expected in the future. **Note: this was an Old Testament ritual.** This is not the peace we will be speaking of here.

Today we define peace as a time of quietness, or the absence of turmoil, confusion or war.

Peace, is often seen for its external value, viewed most as a physical act, usually brought about by two or more opposing or warring forces to end hostility.

The peace Jesus is referring to is not an external one, but internal and spiritual.

It would suffice us to say, you cannot have peace if you don't understand how it comes about, maintained or how it's manifested. And although there are people who believe that somehow, we can manufacture peace through fear and manipulation, that kind of peace is, **1)** not real, and **2)**, it will not last because it is based on deception.

The peace that Jesus refers to is the peace of God that surpasses all fleshly understanding. And the peace he refers to is able to keep our hearts and minds through Christ (Philippians.4: 7).

In the book of Colossians, Paul reminds the believers to let, that is allow, and surrender to the peace of God in their hearts, as they were called to be one in the body of Christ, and be thankful (Colossians.3: 15).

Again, we see this is not an external issue, but an internal spiritual matter.

Why is such focus placed on the internal works of peace? Peace, is mentioned third, in order of the nature or attributes of the Holy Spirit's fruit. Paul tells us it is one of the nine qualities of the Holy Spirit in Galatians (Galatians.5: 22, 23).

Please understand this does not mean or suggest that as believers we can have one, two, or a couple of the fruit of the Spirit.

Look carefully at what it says there, it states, BUT THE "FRUIT" not "FRUITS" of the Spirit is. In other words When the Holy Spirit comes into the believers lives he brings full equipment with him. That is everything we need in order to accomplish the mission of God is brought to us and placed inside us by the Holy Spirit.

We must simply learn how to put into effect what we have been given. Remember Jesus said, that the Holy Spirit would guide us, and teach us, and bring all things he, (the Word of God, Christ), said to our memory (John.14: 26; 16: 13, 14).

We live in a time of confusion, wars and hatred; there is no true peace, only threats, fear and violence. What we call peace is global nuclear fear. It's how other nations are kept in check, because they don't want to be destroyed by bombings or other means. But now they also have the same capabilities, so is this peace?

In Jesus' time, Rome was the threat, they had come in, and set themselves up as the authority in the land, and judgment would be controlled by them.

Jesus was seen as the hope of Israel, he appeared to be the Savior they were told would come in prophecy, Jesus stood up to the injustices of his day, and this would also be against the religious doctrines.

The kingdom they were expecting was not forthcoming as many had anticipated; some were seeking a revolt, such as Barabbas, and Judas. They were ready to make war and have physical confrontations to overcome Roman rule.

Jesus instead spoke of changing one's heart, getting the inside cleaned up and spiritual change. This is not what many following Jesus had hoped for; they were looking for a deliverer like Moses, who would lead them to the promise land, and fulfill scripture.

Jesus in his doctrine wanted his disciples to modify their thinking as well. He lets them know some unknown facts, and that was what's to come for them. Being with him and serving him, was going to come with a price for each of them, even some external peace.

The cross loomed ever larger and closer. In that hour of the last supper, a solemn occasion, would be a time of some final instructions, warnings and encouragement.

The peace Jesus speaks of comes by way of the Comforter, the Holy Spirit, Jesus continues to say his peace is not the same peace that the world gives, and this peace is not temporal but eternal. It would be a peace that the world could not understand. A peace that would, in spite of circumstances remains spiritually intact.

The peace that Jesus spoke of would keep the believers in their darkest times, their hours of despair, and in their times of tribulation (John.16: 33). This is truly HOLY SPIRIT PEACE.

God's peace does not cause us to fear or falter but remain faithful. The peace of our Lord Jesus Christ gives us power to overcome the world, and to remain ever faithful to Him.

God designed us to seek and be with him. He put a part of himself in every living creature, it's his breath of life (Genesis.1:21, 24; 2: 7). It remains connected to him, and at our death, that breath of life goes back to the one who gave it (Ecclesiastes.12: 7).

The peace that man seeks can only be realized once he is back in fellowship and harmony with his creator.

Two-Edge Sword

(Double Trouble)

I believe one of the most profound statements made is found in the book of Hebrews, I quote, *the word of God is quick, and powerful, and shaper than any two edged sword, piercing even to the dividing asunder the soul and spirit, and the joint and marrow, and is a discerner of the thoughts and intents of the heart* (Hebrews.4: 12).

This statement seems to me very military in nature, and although metaphorically speaking, it makes a very clear point (*no pun intended*). We don't know who the writer of this book was, even though there are many speculations surrounding its authorship. A matter that is not worth all the debates given it. One thing is certain, the writer did not mix words, but got to the issues and addressed them promptly as it concerned the saints.

One of those issues, was the matter of the power of God's word. Here it is said to be like a two edged or double-sided sword. It has the power to cut both ways, and pardon me for being blunt, it will cut going in, as well as coming out of its victim.

The sword in its day could inflict tremendous damage on a person through violence (*swords varied in shapes and sizes, as well as length depending on the culture*). A sword could also represent a kingdom by its bearer.

Why is it here said to be a two edged sword? We have seen many times in scripture the use of the sword, they too, could have been two sided. But the writer here put special emphasis on its sharpness and being double sided. The word of God is compared to a double-sided killing tool.

The interesting thing here is this; the word of God is not about being all friendly and cozy with the enemy, (the world).

Believers are told to come out from among them (the worldly, carnal and given to the flesh), and to be separate from them (II Corinthians.6: 17).

We are also told, being friends with the world (carnally minded) is to be an enemy of God (James.4: 4). In other words, worldliness is being in rebellion towards God.

From this point on, the interpretation will get continuously tougher for some readers, as they will discover that the word of God (Jesus' doctrine), is indeed sharper than a two-edged sword.

We are told the word of God is quick, which means it's sudden, it strikes are quick and almost unnoticeable. Quick here also means alive. God's word is alive, God's word is Christ. In the beginning was the Word, the Word was with God, and the Word, was God (John.1: 1). "Christo's" is "The Logo's", Christ is the living word.

The enemy often overcomes the believers like a thief in the night, because saints are sleeping when they should be watching. As Jesus was in the garden of Gethsemane praying to his father, he asked his disciples to watch as he went a little further into the garden to pray (Matthew.26: 37, 38).

Ultimately, they fell asleep, not once but three times, and the last time they were awaken by all the noise of soldiers seeking to arrest Jesus.

Peter who was carrying a sword rose and tried to defend the Lord (Matthew.26: 51, 52). The sword is a weapon, one made for defense, as we see in the case of Peter and Malcus (Mark.14: 47; Luke.22: 50; John.18: 10). It was here used at the wrong time, and for the wrong reason.

Jesus also issues a warning to those who would use the sword. If they were to live by violent means, they would also die by violent means as well. As the sword can be used to defend another's life, it can also be used to take one as well, as this was Peter's intent.

Jesus did not say that Peter was wrong to have a sword, but only that it was wrong of him to put immediate trust in it, and attempting to save a life, and take a life, one that he had no understanding of.

Jesus let them all know, all he had to do was pray, and his Father would send him all the protection he would need (Matthew.26: 53).

The writer of the book of Hebrews likens the word of God to a sword, but with double edges. If it is rightly divided, the word of God cuts those who hear it, as well as those who are delivering it.

The word of God in the hands of an experienced (spiritually minded) Saint, has power. To enter into a battle, one must be equipped; they need to go through boot camp. In other words, saints need to know the basics, and gain PERSONAL SPIRITUAL EXPERIENCE.

Look at what Paul tells the Ephesian Saints, he tells them to put on the whole (complete) armor of God, a soldier is never sent into battle ill prepared. Put on the whole armor of God that you may be able to stand, in other words be prepared to take some blows, some will be wounded, but get back up again, against the wiles (tricks, plots, deceptions, cunning) of the devil. Paul goes on to say we, (the Lords saints) wrestle not against flesh and blood (Ephesians.6: 10-17).

The enemy we face physically, is not the true enemy, for he is unseen to the natural eyes. Satan, like the Lord, uses physical human beings to accomplish his will (deeds) on earth; the warfare is a spiritual one, and fought over the human soul. Let's look briefly at the believer's armor.

This armor is a must have for all believers to have on, and not just in their possession, that would be like having the bible around, and never reading it, or applying it. That would make it no more than decoration.

There is a spiritual war going on, and the Saints of God must take it very seriously. Satan is not playing games, and he is not taking prisoners, a soul lost is condemned to eternal separation from God.

This is one reason even as a young man Jesus said to his family, I must be about my Fathers business (Luke.2: 49), this was not disrespect but focus, at the age of 12 Jesus knew his mission.

Peter tells us, that our adversary, our enemy, **Satan is like a roaring lion, going about seeking, and hunting for whom he might devour** (I Peter.5: 8).

Satan seeks to consume, to take full advantage of our weaknesses, remember also these words of

Jesus to his disciples, the spirit is willing, but the flesh is weak (Matthew.26: 41; Mark.14: 38).

They that are in the flesh (carnal, earthly, and sensually minded) cannot please God (Romans.8: 8).

A spiritual war requires spiritual armor, and you can't obtain this uniform from any store on earth, it has to be given to you from God, and it's guaranteed to fit.

David was going out to meet Goliath, and king Saul offered him his personal armor, David tried it on, but it would not fit, it was not made for him (I Samuel.17: 38, 39).

A spiritual war requires spiritual gear. David relied on the known experience he had with the Lord, and God's power to deliver, as he had done before from the lion and the bear (I Samuel.17: 37).

David went before Goliath wearing the whole spiritual armor of God, and he did so with boldness. **There are no cowards in the Lord's army**. If called upon to do so, we must be willing to forsake all for the kingdom sake (Luke.9: 62), and be willing to die if need be, for our friends (John.15: 13; I John.3: 16).

To follow Jesus will cost something, He said if we are going **to follow him we must be willing to deny ourselves, take up our cross** and follow him

(Luke.9: 23). This means you might have to lose a job, walk away from some friends, or abandon a lifestyle you have grown accustomed to.

Many more people would have followed Christ, if he would have simply let them follow him in their own way.

There was a multitude of people following Jesus because he fed them, it cost them nothing but a little of their time, and they were willing to give it, to get something free. But **Jesus stopped them, and challenged them** by saying, that they needed to move deeper with their relationship, if they were going to continue with him.

Jesus told them, they would have to eat of his flesh, and drink of his blood to remain with him (John.6: 48-66), THE SWORD (Word), MADE SOME DEEP CUTS, so deep were the cuts, that many right then and there, turned away.

Jesus was asking too much of them, they sought physical food, when Jesus said the Spirit quickens (gives life), food sustains the body but not the soul.

The word of God can give life, or it can also take it. There is no true life, apart from the Word of God. *Man shall not live by bread alone but by every word that comes from the mouth of God* (Matthew.4: 4; Luke.4: 4).

The Gospel divides family and friends. Jesus made a tough statement when it comes to service, he said he was sending a fire on earth, and that his teaching would cause division among people (Luke.12: 49-53).

Jesus' teaching would cause the father to be against the son, and son against father. And children against parents, as well as in-laws. The gospel will not often bring physical families together, but it was going to build spiritual families. The sword of the gospel divides homes and all who are in them.

The world is considered dead (spiritually), without Christ. And as we have already pointed out, this was the first part of death when Adam sinned in the garden.

Man, became spiritually estranged from God. Consider the following, a young man was invited to follow the Lord one day, and the promising new disciple requested that he first be permitted to go (remain where he was, and wait until his father died and was buried, then he would follow).

Jesus simply said, follow him, and let the dead (spiritually) bury the dead (physically). Matthew.8: 21, 22.

The teachings of Christ went far beyond being a morally conscious individual as man teaches. Jesus' doctrine was focused on inner spiritual change, brought about by ones surrender to God, by the power of the Holy Spirit.

To be likeminded people means getting along, we are told to let the mind of Christ be our guides (Philippians.2: 5).

Debates, arguments and confusion come by way of disagreements, and lack of unity. John tells us that there are three that agree in Heaven, the Father, the Word and the Holy Ghost (I John.5: 7). In order for there to be healing, there has to be a wounding first. Sin has wounded mankind.

When we are spiritually cut with the word of God, we are then put in position to become what the Lord had designed us to be.

Isaiah records the words of God saying, *come now let us reason together says the Lord, though your sins be as scarlet, they shall be white as snow, though they be red like crimson they shall be as wool, the Lord goes on to say, if you are **WILLING AND OBEDIENT** you shall eat the fat of the land, but if you **REFUSE AND REBEL** you shall be devoured with the sword, for the mouth of the Lord has spoken it* (Isaiah.1:18-20).

Sin is the wound that cannot be cured by any other means than the blood of Christ. He (Christ), was wounded for our transgressions, he was bruised for our iniquities, and the chastisement of our peace was upon him, and with HIS STRIPES WE ARE HEALED (Isaiah.53: 5).

The word of God cuts believers and nonbelievers alike, but be assured also, he can heal both as well.

Come Out Wherever You Are

The call of Christ is the call of duty, it's a call of commitment, and focus. It's a call that many hear, but only a few responds to. The call of Christ is a call of separation, and at times even isolation.

Being obedient to Christ means LEAVING THINGS BEHIND in the world. Saints are reminded, not to love the world, or the things of the world, and that if anyone loves the world, the love of the Father is not in them (I John.2: 15). We have read that the sword will cut both ways, and as sinful creatures, we want to take others along with us, believing we can convince them to change, the longer they are around us.

Believers are told to come out from among them (spiritually corrupt), and be separate (II Corinthians.6: 14-17). In other words, the new life lived in Christ, should be clearly visible to others. As it is said in Matthew.5: 16, it is allowing the light of Christ to shine from within us, to those around us, so that they will see our good (Godly) works, and glorify God in Heaven.

Furthermore, we are told to have no fellowship with the unfruitful works of darkness (Ephesians.5: 11). What are the unfruitful works of darkness; they are the works or desires of the flesh, as found in Galatians 5: 19-21(read also Romans.1: 18-32).

From the first century, until this 21 century, there is a great tolerance for sin. But that does not mean it is acceptable to God. God loves the sinner; this is why he sent his Son Jesus, to die for sin. But make no mistake about it, **GOD HATES SIN**.

As Saints of God, we are in the world but not of the world, we are a holy nation, a royal priesthood, even a peculiar people called by God (I Peter.2: 9). We are called to be ambassadors for Christ (II Corinthians.5: 20). And called to represent the Lord on his behalf. To share his gospel with the world, by way of our own personal testimonies, and experiences with him, to be always ready to give a reason for the hope we have in Christ (I Peter.3: 15).

Let's be clear, this is not about us, the Holy Spirit was given that we would be witnesses of Jesus by way of the gospel. The Spirit brings to our minds the things that will bring Glory to God, and not ourselves (John.16: 13-15). When Cornelius tried to worship Peter, he was quickly told by Peter that he (Peter) was just a man like him (Acts.10: 25, 26).

Jesus came to earth to bring unity, but before that can be done there has to first be a purging, and a spiritual cleansing. Attitudes had to change, if actions were going to be adjusted. Man had to see himself in the true light. Jesus is the light of the world (John.1: 1-5). In Christ, is no darkness at all (I John.1: 5). But, the scriptures tell us, people loved darkness, deception, trickery rather than light (John.3: 19).

Knowing this is true, how do we get people to come out of sin, and away from darkness? Jesus did everything as an example; it was done to show what needs to be done as well as how it's possible to be done, even while living in these fleshly bodies.

We must deal with sin, but in order to do so, we must recognize it as real, and accept what God has said about us, and our nature to sin. We cannot walk in the newness of God's light put inside us, until we get rid of the old mindset of sin through a surrendered life. We must come out from among the worldly things of this life, and be separate, and available unto the Lord for his glory.

The Gospel

What is the gospel? It's called the good news. So, those who seek the gospel, want to hear some good news. We have as a culture of people, grown accustomed to what we say is a positive vibe, and feeling. People want to be made to feel good, I'm okay you're okay, and you're okay, and I'm okay.

Feelings are not the best way to be assured of things in life. Feelings are good, but we should be careful not to be led, or possibly misled by them. Feelings can cause us to be stirred up positively. But, they can also lead us down the path of disappointment, and feelings of negativity.

Feelings can be based on false, or perceived experiences that may have never occurred. Feelings can bolster strong desires, real or imagined. Feelings often gain strength by emotions, and as I have already stated, people want to be made to feel good.

How does all this tie into the gospel? We will do our best to explain it. Take into consideration what you have learned thus far about the two-edged sword, and the living word.

Jesus began his ministry by proclaiming the gospel of the Kingdom (Matthew.4: 23; 11: 5; 24: 14).

Was this a different gospel than the one we are most familiar with? No, in the time of kings and kingdoms these words spoken by Jesus were very timely.

Jesus' words let his audience know that change was now underway, and that he was preaching a new kingdom, with new leadership being at hand. This statement made by Jesus was one the Jews knew well, since they had a history of kings and kingdoms. This gospel was also known as the gospel of Jesus Christ, the Son of God (Mark.1: 1; 16: 15).

This same gospel is the gospel of redemption (Luke.4: 18, 19; 7: 22). Jesus' gospel ministry was filled with signs and wonders (miracles). These actions were attention getters, used much in the same way the Lord used the burning bush to get Moses' attention, demonstrating the power and the glory of God.

Before John the Baptist came along, there was over 400 years of silence, and no open visions. John came preaching baptism and repentance, and that someone was coming, who would set things right. Jesus now comes along proclaiming the gospel of the kingdom, being baptized by John. Jesus was led into the wilderness to be tempted by Satan. He returned in power, having authority from God the Father to restore and redeem mankind.

The good news came in the form of a man, Jesus the Christ. Inside that man, was totally God. In him (Christ), dwells the fullness of the Godhead bodily (Colossians.2: 9).

The prophecies were being fulfilled by Christ daily, and the words he spoke in the Temple, he was a living example of them. The gospel was living among them, in the person of Jesus Christ.

Jesus preached the gospel of the kingdom, the gospel of change. But his teaching was internal first. If things around us are to change, then things inside us has to change first. A kingdom needs people, the right kind of people. Jesus said to his disciples that unless they become as little children, they would not enter into the Kingdom (Matthew.18: 1-4). Jesus' focus was on the hearts of men. Changed hearts, brings changed attitudes and actions.

The power of the gospel is in the people it affects, the gospel is medicine to those who are sick. Jesus said, *they that are whole have no need of a physician but they that are sick, he goes on to say, he did not come to call the righteous but sinners to repentance* (Luke.5: 31, 32).

Jesus' medicine affected the internal before it did the external. We must also say that boldness comes with knowing the gospel (to know the gospel is to know the person the gospel is about, by way of salvation). The Apostle Paul is a testament to this, as he was one of the great persecutors of the church until coming to know the Lord by a firsthand experience (Acts chapters 8-9). Paul would give his life to the spread of the gospel to the world.

Paul, a Jew and a Pharisee, became the unthinkable; he became a Christian, a follower of "that way", a servant of Christ, and one of the greatest activists of faith in Christ in the known world.

Listen to what he had to say when he sent a letter to the believers at Rome, *I am not ashamed of the gospel of Christ, for it is the power of God unto salvation unto everyone that believes, to the Jew first and also unto the Greek (Gentiles)*. Romans.1: 16.

Here was a man who came from a powerful ancestral and religious background, a man who learned and knew the law better than most Jews, he was a Pharisee, and the son of a Pharisee (Acts.23: 6), and Paul was familiar with all things Jewish.

Saul (later called Paul), the man who held the coats of those who stoned one of the Lords saints, had an unexpected personal visit from the head of the church himself; it was a life changing and life altering experience. I don't know of anyone who has been in the presence of God that walked away unchanged. Even if it's in disagreement with Christ, his principles and practices.

The gospel has power, and the gospel is power. What is the gospel? It's not that Jesus was born in a stable, or that he grew up in Jerusalem, the gospel is not that Jesus went about doing good or even healing the sick, feeding multitudes or raising the dead, all these were simply a part of who he was, but there were people who did many of the things he had done before Jesus came on the scene, and even since he has ascended back to Heaven.

What makes this gospel so good is this, it can again be found in something the Apostle Paul said, and it's found in I Corinthians 15: 3, 4 and it reads like this, *for I delivered unto you first of all that which I also received, how Christ died for our sins according to scripture and that he was buried, and that he rose again the third day according to scripture.*

What sets Jesus' ministry apart is, he not only died, but he rose again from the dead, just as he said he would. What set Jesus apart from all those who came before or after him, is his claim to be the Son of God, and he demonstrated this in power, and practice. Jesus claimed to be sent from God to deliver those who were oppressed, sick, and downhearted, was that good news, it certainly is to me, how about you? The gospel of Jesus Christ breaks the shackles of sin, and by faith removes the penalty that accompanied it.

The Christian faith is set apart because the believers do not worship their founder as one who came into the world, did some wonderful works, and gave some great speeches, then died. The gospel we put our hope in, rest in the power of Jesus rising from the dead.

The gospel, as the saints of God know it, gives power to those who put their trust in the promises and the finished work of Jesus Christ.

Radical Relationship

What does the Lord expect from his followers? He expects the same from each of them. First, it is to become familiar with Him (Jesus), and that cannot be done apart from learning the scriptures that the Holy Spirit will open up to us, as we yield ourselves to him.

The very first thing Jesus instructs his disciples to do (those who had been with him for the three years of his ministry), was to tarry (wait), in Jerusalem until they receive power from on high, Heaven (Luke.24: 49). When they receive this power, in the person of the Holy Spirit (Acts.1: 8), they would become WITNESSES for Christ.

A witness is one that tells what he or she has seen or experienced firsthand, but to ensure that they did not just go about saying anything or just doing what they wanted to do, the Holy Spirit would guide them into all truth and bringing back to their memory **all things Jesus had said and done** (John.16: 13).

As believers and Saints of God, we have a very unique relationship with him by way of his Son. We are now, because of Jesus offering himself up as the final sacrifice required by God, been moved and allowed back into the throne room of the Almighty.

We once again have full access, to the PARADISE OF GOD.

Early in his ministry Jesus' disciples were seen as servants, but as he was preparing to go back to the Father he no longer called them servants since a servant he said, did not know what his master does (John.15: 15). Jesus now calls them friends, please take special note how the Lord calls Judas the one who would betray him, FRIEND also (Matthew.26: 50).

Jesus lifts the disciples up to a new level of relationship by now calling them friends. He was saying to them you are not slaves you are my brothers. Jesus was speaking of equality and equal importance.

Paul said as believers we are heirs and joint heirs with Christ (Romans.8: 17).

What Satan meant for evil God meant for good. Christ death on the cross and resurrection brought us back together, God and man. The eviction notice given to Adam was paid in full and redeemed by the Lord Jesus Christ, Satan had no choice but to give the deed over to the one he could not corrupt, and the one death could not hold (Revelation.1: 18).

This new relationship would not be based on genealogical ties; it would have its power in the Blood of Christ and redemption by the cross. It was from that very cross that Jesus makes this point clear, saying to his mother, woman behold your son (referring to the disciple John), and son behold your mother (referring to Mary), and we are told from that hour John took her in (John.19: 26, 27).

As Jesus sat and taught one day, he was informed that his mother, and his brothers wanted to see him, Jesus posed a question to those in the room asking, who is my mother and my brothers? I'm sure there were no shortage of confused looks.

Jesus stretched his arms out and said look around, here is my mother and my brothers, and anyone who does the will of my Father in Heaven, the same is my brother, my sister, and mother (Matthew.12: 47-50).

Jesus was letting them all know, not to put EARTHLY RELATIONSHIPS before their SPIRITUAL RELATIONSHIP with God.

Before our redemption, we were the creation of God, and his handiwork, but that was never enough to restore man back to God.

We have the joy of knowing, that when we accept Christ as our Savior, we become sons and daughters of God by the new birth. For as many as received him (Christ), to them gave he power to become the sons, (spiritual children), of God, even to those who believes on his name (John.1: 12).

We now have a spiritual relationship linked to all believers by Christ blood, and the presence of the Holy Spirit.

We can all be brothers and sisters in Christ as we have been washed in his blood and made spiritually whole. What makes this radical is there are no barriers between those who are in the body of Christ, no Jews and Gentiles, bond or free (I Corinthians.12: 13).

We are all family in Jesus Christ by his blood and have all been made to drink of the Spirit.

Our relationship with God has nothing to do with the color of our skin or genealogical background. It is solely based on our confession of faith in Christ.

The War is On!

We looked at what happened to David when he tried on another man's armor, it did not fit him properly. It's possible to go out and try to face the enemy based on what we have heard can be done, or possibly has been done by someone else. But be advised, the enemy knows you better than you think.

One such an example of this, is the men who thought to cast out demons in the New Testament. There were some Jews who had witnessed the miraculous hand of God at work through the Apostle Paul, (Acts.19: 11-13). And because these Jewish men did not know the Lord, what they saw and believed, was that Paul was doing these miracles in his own power, so they thought to imitate him.

There are many people who don't want to surrender themselves to the Lord, but they want the blessings that go with being faithful to him can bring. These men were known to be exorcist might have had some measure of success fooling the people, and they took it upon themselves to go into a situation they knew nothing about.

Maybe there was safety in numbers as there were 7 of them, and they were sons of priest (Acts.19: 14) which also suggest they should have known the power of God's word. But knowing what the word of God says does not qualify anyone for miracles.

And if that wasn't bad enough, they did not go in facing these demons with faith. They instead told the demons to come out of this man, in the name of Jesus, whom Paul preaches (Acts.19: 13). These men dared to go to war without counting the cost, and without knowing what they were doing. The evil spirit now challenges them saying, Jesus I know, and Paul I know, but who are you (v.15)?

Big mistake on their part, the man who had the evil spirit, now was really upset. One man with evil spirits can overcome seven men, who were pretenders. The man with demons in him, jumped on them, and beat them, overcoming them and they ran from the house naked and wounded (v.16). What a stark difference with what happened with Jesus when he was met by the man in the graveyard who had demons.

This man was naked, and cutting himself with stones (Mark.5: 1-15). Here was a man possessed with demons, but recognized Jesus, and was afraid of him. Here is another clear picture of the world's colliding, the battle of the spirit world and the physical world.

There is a war between good (God) and evil (Satan). What's at stake is man's eternal soul; the human body is merely where the battles are waged.

The man in the graveyard was only acting out what was taking place inside him, there was chaos, confusion, anger, etc., and the demons wanted this man to destroy himself by causing harm to his body. His spiritual war was having physical affects (*It must be said at this point that every condition we see is not the result of Satan or demons, some are caused by biological imbalances that medication is required*).

There are things killing us not because we did something wrong personally, an example of this is the man born blind in John chapter 9. Jesus said his blindness was not due to something he or his parents had done, his blindness was so God could demonstrate his love for us.

Doctors are needed, not just to be seen as decorations, the Lord uses them also to help cure, and heal our bodies, that's the physical side of life. But the soul needs healing as well, and when the soul is out of sync the body is usually also troubled, as we find here. This man was a tortured individual, but with all that was taking place inside, he still knew where to get help.

This war is a soul to soul war; it rages within all of us, Paul speaking to the Roman Saints tells them there is always a war in his members (mentality, the mind), a war in our inward (spiritual) man, (Romans.7:

23). Doing battle against what our flesh, (old nature) wants us to do.

Jesus was fulfilling his call and ministry to heal the broken hearted, and to set at liberty those who are bruised. Jesus came to face Satan; to let him know that his little kingdom was about to come an end. That his hold on mankind would be completely broken shortly. When the seventy returned rejoicing Jesus was heard to say, *I beheld Satan fall like lightening from heaven* (Luke.10: 18).

Jesus cast the demons out of the man in the graveyard, and the man is seen sitting at the feet of Jesus clothed and in his right mind (Mark.5: 15). Physical wars come because of spiritual confusion. Where there is envying and strife there is confusion and every evil work (James.3: 16).

Everyone has to choose a side, Joshua speaking to Gods people Israel, charged them to make a decision, to choose who they would serve, whether it would be the true and living God, who has always delivered them, or the false gods of Egypt (Joshua.24: 15, 16).

James asked the question (Chapter 4: 1), from where does wars (strong disagreements) and fighting's come from among you (the believers)? He was pointing out to them that this happens when people are walking in their flesh. We know that they that are in the flesh, (walking according to fleshly desires) cannot please God (Romans.8: 8).

If you are going to join the Lord's army, you must be sure you are ready for what's about to come. We must not make the mistake of going off to war, and not fully prepared to do so. The whole armor of God must be worn, this is where so many believers lose against the enemy. They think they are ready because they have memorized a few scriptures and go to church regularly.

It will take more than having a zeal (strong desire) for God's word, to deal with the enemy. We are at war with Satan, but it should also be said that some of your greatest battles, will be with your own fleshly desires.

The Whole Armor of God

The Apostle Paul was a soldier in the army of the Lord, but before that I believe he was a crusader for Judaism, he was a man acquainted with the Law, and was himself also a Pharisee. It was said that he sat at the feet of one of the great teachers at that time Gamaliel learning the law (Acts.22: 3).

Paul was so into Judaism that when he learned of those who had seemingly forsaken and abandoning its teachings, he was enraged, and wanted to do what he could to protect their way of life, to assist God in bringing these heathens to justice. Individuals who were violating the Laws of Moses. But never knowing that he would have a talk with the one who gave the Law to Moses, and in Acts 22, Paul would testify of the events that led to his conversion.

Paul was well qualified to speak on the matters of the Law, but he was only getting half the picture, until he met Christ on the road to Damascus. Paul's heart burned within him against all those who opposed Judaism. It didn't matter to him, man, woman, or child, as a loyal soldier he went into battle mode, and would bring as many back to Jerusalem as he could, to face death (Acts.9: 1-3).

Paul was the soldier's soldier, a leader who was not afraid to be on the front-line to meet the enemy head on. He showed no fear, and 100 % allegiance to Judaism.

Paul had with him a band of soldiers who were under his command, who were likewise ready to do what they had to against this uprising and revolt. Paul had on the whole armor, and at that time he was not wearing the armor God would later replace his with. But let's look at the basic armor that soldiers wore. (*Please forgive me for not going into great archaeological details about the equipment worn; my descriptions are only for basic information of what they wore as described in Ephesians chapter 6*).

When Paul was converted, he took those experiences he had as a soldier, and applied them to his new walk in Christ, and in his letter to the Saints at Ephesus, he uses a metaphor when he spoke of the equipment the believers would need to do battle against evil and Satan. It was a uniform they were all familiar with; they had all seen Roman soldiers before, since they were under the authority of Rome.

Paul was accustomed to what it took to be a soldier for Rome, now in this letter to the Ephesians, he lets the Saints know what it was going to take to be a spiritual soldier for the Lord Jesus Christ. He lets them know, that if they are to be victorious, there's a few things they must do, and on the very top of the list was, BE STRONG IN THE LORD and the power of his might, putting on the whole armor of God. He tells them, that they may stand against the wiles (deceptions, tricks) of the devil (Ephesians.6: 10, 11).

Rome was also considered the devil at that time, and later in Revelations called the great whore of Babylon (Revelations.17:5-13). Bear in mind that Rome, Caesar in particular, did not believe in God, but called himself god. So, to resist Caesar, was in effect to resist god.

So, the war being fought, was being done on two fronts, the physical, as well as the spiritual, as Paul relates to them, (the Saints), we wrestle not against flesh and blood *only*, but against principalities, against powers, against the rulers of this world, against spiritual wickedness in high places (Ephesians.6: 12).

Paul knew what they would have to face and war against, because he was once the face of Rome; he was once the enemy of the faith. Who better to stir the troops than Paul, first he lets them know they must know God, and second, they must know their enemy if they were to be successful in overcoming and defeating him? Today some would see Paul as a defector, changing sides midstream and bringing all the enemies secrets and shortcomings to the other side. This was another reason those in power at Rome wanted to have Paul eliminated, HE KNEW TO MUCH.

Jesus said, you can't take over the house until you bind the strong man of the house (Matthew.12: 23-29; Mark.3: 22-27). He was referring to Satan being the resident strong man whose house (power) is taken from him, when another (Christ), came along and cast him out.

Jesus said all power (authority) is given to him, in Heaven and earth (Matthew.28: 18), and that he has the keys of Hell and death (Revelation.1: 18).

Remember what we said earlier about the lease or deed. Because of the work of Christ, it no longer belongs to Satan. The work of Christ is done never having to be done again. But there is a spiritual war for the soul of man that rages on, until the return of Christ to set up his kingdom on earth.

How do we overcome and defeat the evil one, Satan and his demons? We must prepare, it's fundamental. Without knowledge of God's word by application, we will lose, in other words we must walk by faith, not by sight. Because our enemy appears to be stronger than us, does not mean he is. Greater is he (The Holy Spirit) that is in you, than he (the ungodly, spirit of Antichrist) that is in the world (I John.4: 4).

Paul lets the saints know there will be a fight, and not all victories will be easy. He lets them know they would have to withstand, tolerate, endure, put up with, and go through much for some victories. There will be casualties, as there is with any war, but Paul admonishes them to remain standing faithful (Ephesians.6: 13).

Paul begins to break down the armor of their spiritual warfare uniform. Going to war takes planning. Jesus asked what king going to make war against another king, does not first make plans to see if his 10 thousand men will be able to go against the 20 thousand men of his enemy (Luke.14: 31).

The spiritual army is always greater than the natural or physical army. Jesus in the garden when they came to arrest him Peter tried to defend him with the physical sword, he was told by the Lord to put it away. Jesus said if he wanted to, he could pray to the Father, and he would send him more than 12 legions of angels to defend him (Matthew26: 50-53).

In the book of II Kings, the king of Syria wanted to know where the prophet of God was who was giving his information out, that none should have known. He sent spies to find where Elisha was staying, and the king sent an army to bring him back. He was in Dothan. The King wanted him brought back, and soldiers surrounded the city at night. The young man who was with Elisha, went out early in the morning and saw the army, and woke Elisha panicking asking what will they do?

Elisha's answer was not what the young man expected, he said fear not, for they that are with us are more than those with them. Elisha prayed to the Lord, to open the young man's eyes to see, and what was revealed to him was a mountain full of horses and chariots of fire (II Kings.6: 11-17). The army that accompanies the saints always outnumbers those of the enemies of God.

As believers, our spiritual sight must be clearer than our natural sight. Put on the

BREASTPLATE OF RIGHTEOUSNESS

Paul says, it is one of the first parts of the outer armor; it covers the vital organs against attack as seen in the picture (*most armor did not cover the back of the soldier and the reason for this was clear, in the ranks of the soldiers there was always another soldier following close behind them, in other words they had one another's back*).

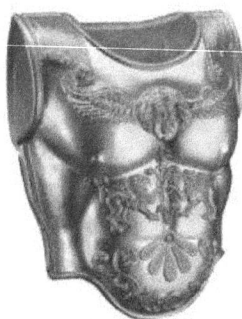

I equate righteousness with holiness. Job said, *I put on righteousness and it clothed me, my judgment was a robe and a diadem* (Job.29: 14).

The breastplate is our holiness or soul protection. It protects the heart which was known as the center of man's life. The Lord speaking to Abraham of the promised inheritance to come through him by faith, believed God, and it was counted to Abraham for righteousness or holiness (Genesis15: 4-6).

Roman soldiers were not known for retreating, they were known to overwhelm their enemy, often with sheer numbers alone. The breastplate of the believers is forged from the very holiness of God. Paul goes on to say, having your **FEET SHOD WITH THE PREPARATION OF THE GOSPEL OF PEACE. The steps of a good (godly) man** are ordered (directed) by the Lord (Psalms.27: 23). The word of the Lord is a lamp unto my feet, and light unto our path (Psalms.119: 105).

How beautiful upon the mountain are the feet of him that brings good tidings (Isaiah.52: 7).

The gospel is good news, but it will not be easy to convey this message of peace to a sinful world. A world that has gone after wickedness and given to sin.

The enemy will defend its rebellious ways, to justify itself. Like we said earlier, the gospel is good news, but it will divide homes and lives, and it will cut everyone it encounters.

The wicked will fight back, Paul tells the believers to take with them

THE SHIELD OF FAITH, and with it they can quench all the fiery darts of the wicked. The shield was a tool to protect the one who carries it from outside attacks.

Its call the shield of faith, it's what the believer trust will keep them safe against their adversary.

Paul used his shield on a few occasions, particularly when the saints did not believe he was truly converted, when they were afraid because of his past deeds (Acts.9).

One of Satan's greatest weapons against us, is our past, and our shield of faith guards us from spiritual harm that the enemy seeks to cause based on our past. David said, the Lord is my strength and my shield (Psalms.28: 7).

Consider this also, your shield can be used to protect another soldier from harm, from someone who wants to use their past mistakes against them to you. Believers are to guard one another, if one falls the bible tells us, those who are spiritual among us should restore such a one (Galatians.6: 1), being careful that we don't fall ourselves into temptation.

Our faith can become the strength of another. As Jesus was teaching one day, a group of men brought their sick friend to see him, but they could not get near Jesus, because there were so many people in the house he was teaching in.

This man's friends were not going to give up, what they did next was amazing. They climbed on the roof, and tore it off, and let down their friend for Jesus to heal him (Mark.2: 1-5; Luke.5: 18-20).

The shield of faith can protect even those who don't know they need protecting.

Take also **THE HELMET OF SALVATION**.

It's small but carries the greatest power. The body gets its orders from the head, and if something happens to the head, the whole body suffers because of it.

Faith comes by hearing, and hearing the word of God (Romans.10: 17). Salvation comes by the acknowledgment of Christ as our Savior. For by grace are you saved through faith, and that not of yourselves, it is the gift of God not of works, lest any man should boast (Ephesians.2: 8, 9).

The head of our Faith is Christ, who is also the head of the Church (Colossians1: 17-19), which is his body (spiritual representative) on earth, and the gates of hell cannot prevail against it (Matthew.16: 18). In Christ there is life. The helmet of salvation is also the helmet of life, because wearing it, could possibly save the life of that individual.

Take also **THE SWORD OF THE SPIRIT** which is the word of God. We have looked at, and spoke about the two-edged sword, and what it can do. In order to be effective in the war against Satan, the flesh, and sin, it means that we must be Spirit fed and spirit led. Filled with, and rooted in God's word. David said thy word have I hid in my heart that I might not sin against thee (Psalms.119: 11). Every word of God is pure he is a shield unto them that put their trust in Him (Proverbs.30: 5).

In the beginning was the Word, and the Word was with God, and the Word was God. Paul told Timothy to study, to show himself approved unto God, a workman who needed not be ashamed, and rightly dividing the word of truth (II Timothy.2: 15). which means cut it straight, and tell the truth. A soldier is to weld his sword in power, with one purpose, and that is to take the enemy out. This was Peter's intent in the Garden when he tried to protect Christ, but Peter like so many of us, did not know what he was doing.

Peter had a weapon in his hand, but no knowledge or understanding of what to do with it. So many individuals handle the word of God in the same way; it's in their hands, but they have no idea what it is, and don't know how it's to be used.

The bible is God's revealed word to the world; it's his road map that leads to Heaven, if it is followed correctly. The Bible is a spiritual book that cannot be understood by those who are fleshly minded. The natural man it's said, receives not the things of God, neither can he know them, because they are spiritually discerned (I Corinthians.2:14).

We are engaged in a war, an everlasting spiritual war for the souls of mankind. Jesus said the harvest is ripe for picking, but the laborers are few (Matthew.9: 37). Even the believers are busy doing what they choose to do, rather than what the Lord has called them to do.

Today fewer people are answering the call of the Lord to service; the focus is on pleasing themselves and getting along with the world.

Jesus said, if anyone will follow him, they must deny themselves, deny their passions, deny their urges, and take up their cross and follow him (Matthew.16: 24-26; Mark.8: 34; Luke.9: 23). Take up sorrows, take up loneliness, and take up family abandonment. Following Christ does not mean it will be easy, in fact it could cost our lives, as it did with many of the Saints before us.

Paul wanted the Saints to know that there is a war going on, and unless you are prepared, you will either be a victim or victorious.

The Roman soldier would be prepared

to give their life for Caesar their king, as he called for them to do when they entered service for Rome. Christ used Rome as one of his examples. When asked should they pay tribute (taxes), Jesus response was, render to Caesar the things that are Caesar's and to God what is God's (Luke.20: 22-25). Paul was a Roman citizen and soldier who came to know Christ. And was set free from himself, from his own prison of his mind. Paul, now a soldier of the Lord, reaped the benefits of applying what he had learned as a Pharisee, and Roman Jew, into teaching others what it would mean to know Jesus as their Lord and Savior, and joining the Lord's army.

Putting on the whole armor of God is necessary, if we are to do battle with the enemy. He (the evil one), is sly, quick and cunning, he looks to find weaknesses in the saints armor, and if he cannot find any there, he will look to find weaknesses in the one who wears the uniform (*by way of fleshly lying witnesses or their unsaved past deeds*).

Paul was skilled in the Law of Judaism, and a master of languages, and that made him a good candidate and soldier for the Lord Jesus Christ.

One of the many things I love about God is this, **He does not always change our direction, or the path we are on. But he will change our desires** and purpose for where we are going, and what we will do when we get there.

The Lord gave each of us talents and skills that can be used to glorify him. Many of us are not using our gifts (talents) for the Lord, as if they belong to us. But if those of us who are in the field of service for the Lord, share the gospel with others, some might come to the Lord, and give their time and talent to Him.

God's good news to us is that His Son has redeemed us back to himself; the mistake Adam made in the Garden, was made right by the blood of Jesus on the cross. The Eviction served to Adam has been cleared up, and cleaned up. And stamped paid in full.

Rebellion drove man from Paradise; the Righteousness of Christ allows us access to Paradise in Heaven, and true fellowship with the Lord once again.

Trouble in the Valley

Your enemy, your adversary, is like a roaring lion going about seeking whom he might devour. Unless we are totally equipped to do battle against Satan, it is not wise to try to stand against him.

In the book of James, the believers are told, to submit themselves unto God and resist the devil and he would flee from them (James.4: 7). Satan often wins small battles because of the unwillingness of those who go out against him to prepare. The people of God will always have their faith challenged and tested to see how real it truly is. The battle between good and evil is ever present. For instance, the battle of David and Goliath is a good example.

David met Goliath, not out of fear, but by faith. He wore no visible armor, and yet he was well armored spiritually, and prepared to do battle against this sinful giant.

David did not trust what his eyes saw, but rather what his faith knew, and his experience had taught him about God.

David did not go out trying to impress anyone, he just knew he could not let this heathen continue to blaspheme his God, and nothing be done about it.

Was David concerned about Goliath's size, weight or reputation? No more than he was concerned about the power of the lion, or the strength of the bear he defended his flock against? **David knew the power of his God**, and went to meet the one who dared think he was a giant before God.

King Saul was afraid, as was all his soldiers, they felt small in the sight of this hulk of a Philistine, and David's brothers thought he only wanted to see what was going on, but David was what was going on.

David, appeared as no more than a child in the sight of them all. David was ready to lay down his life for his faith. David had is loins girt about with truth, and had his previous experiences with the Lord's divine protection with him, in the face of trouble and adversity. David wore the breastplate of righteousness,

David served a Holy God who defends to the utmost, and his feet shod with the gospel of peace.

David's actions would bring about the defeat of those who did not believe in God's ability to deliver. The shield of faith was with him as he walked by faith and not by sight. As he walked into the valley and shadow of death to meet this evil giant. For the Lord was with him.

In his heart was that helmet of salvation, the power to overcome the enemy and his sword was one smooth stone that would bring one thought to be mighty to the ground. David trusted the word of God, and the things that he was taught as a young man, things he knew from experience and he felled a giant and took his head.

As God was able to deliver David, he is able to do the same for us; we must trust the Lord with all our hearts and not think that our way is the best way.

David is a good example of putting on the whole armor of God, and how trying to put on what belongs to another, is not how we please the Lord. The armor the Lord has given to each of us, will fit no one but us. And the longer we wear it, in time we will find that it is a perfect fit. The Lord has called each of us to duty, there are people dying daily, people who need to know Jesus loves them, and that God has prepared a place for them in Heaven, even before the foundation of the world.

Each of us has a valley to go through. David penned the 23rd Psalm reminding us, **though we walk through the valley and shadow of death, the Lord is with us, his rod and staff would comfort us**. Just because there might be **trouble in the valley does not mean there will not be peace on the mountain top.**

David did not fear what man could do to him; today we have all the power of the Godhead working within each of us, to give us power over the world, our flesh and Satan.

Be mindful that the Father Loved us (John.3: 16), the Son died for us (John.10: 11-15) and the Spirit seals us (Ephesians.1: 13). So, no matter what comes our way, we are more than capable of dealing with it, as we lean and depend on the Lord.

Jesus said, in this world we shall have tribulations (John.16: 33), **there are some things that are unavoidable,** but that does not mean they cannot be overcome, and how do we overcome the world, our flesh and the devil? By our faith (I John.5: 4).

There are valleys in all our lives, but there are also mountaintops that we can rise to, and stand in the presence of God, and feel his power and rest in his glory.

Conclusion

For I am not ashamed of the gospel of Christ: for it is the power of God unto salvation to every one that believeth; to the Jew first, and also to the Greek (Romans.1: 16).

Everything we do as believers is based on our faith and commitment to the Lord and how we share that faith with others.

In order for us to have continued victory over the world, our flesh and the devil we must be equipped, as we are told to put on the whole armor of God. This is important because, once we accepted Jesus as our savior, we enlisted in God's army, and we now battle against Satan daily. Being joined to the body of Christ means we are now in a spiritual warfare.

Jesus said, he did not come to send peace on earth but a sword, and that the word of God was going to separate people, and the word of God is like a two edged sword (Hebrews.4: 12), cutting both ways.

As saints of God we have a personal responsibility to the body of Christ to share the good news of the Gospel with others, but in doing so, we must be prepared to do this having on the whole armor of God, or our enemy who is like a roaring lion will devour us for our lack of preparedness.

About the Author

Timothy White Sr. has impacted thousands of people throughout the world as an author, teacher, motivational speaker and minister. Mr. White is on a mission to positively influence millions of people through his work, ministry and writing, which currently exceeds 80+ books covering a plethora of topics including bullying, domestic violence, self-help, history and spirituality.

The Cleveland, Ohio native, a father of five, has overcome many adversities in his life including homelessness and losing his beloved wife to cancer in 1994. Through much heartache and disappointments he discovered a new purpose and passion to use writing as a tool to "plant positive seeds."

Mr. White has developed profound spiritual insight into relationships over the years. Mr. White has written multiple books on the topic of abuse including, In the Ring with Heels On, She's the Boss and Victims of Bullies. Mr. White writes about these and other issues because of the relevance, and prevalence of domestic and other violence. He believes that, "Information plus application equals transformation."

Mr. White is an Evangelist and former pastor. He believes, "God chooses who He uses." He writes, speaks, and ministers to local, national, and international audiences. With an additional 15 new books in the works, Mr. White hopes to give people plenty of "spiritual food" to eat.

White is one of the producers of the documentary "Where's Gina?" about missing children on which he was also narrator.

He is a co-developer of a tech company (Gsys LLC) that brought blindside technology to vehicles that made billions for the industry, saving countless lives.

He is currently co-hosting a radio show, " Healing the Hurt" on WERE 1490am in Cleveland, Ohio on Thursday evenings 8-10 pm with Host, Rev. Brenda Ware-Abrams.

He is currently on the Advisory Board and is a volunteer instructor at the Juvenile Correction centers in Warrensville Heights and Cleveland, Ohio where his book Seven Signs of Success is being taught.

His book Victims of Bullies is, currently, in the City of Cleveland School system to help stop and make aware of solutions to the issue of bullying.

timwhite55@gmail.com   Timwhitepublishing.com

www.ingramcontent.com/pod-product-compliance
Lightning Source LLC
Chambersburg PA
CBHW031224090426
42740CB00007B/693